Reflections and Nature Watercolors

Written and Illustrated by

Margaret Kohel Evans

WestBow Press books may be ordered through booksellers or by contacting:

WestBow Press
A Division of Thomas Nelson & Zondervan
1663 Liberty Drive
Bloomington, IN 47403
www.westbowpress.com
844-714-3454

Interior Image Credit: Margaret Kohel Evans

ISBN: 978-1-6642-8311-4 (sc)
ISBN: 978-1-6642-8313-8 (hc)
ISBN: 978-1-6642-8312-1 (e)

Library of Congress Control Number: 2022920468

Print information available on the last page.

WestBow Press rev. date: 11/22/2022

WESTBOW
PRESS®
A DIVISION OF THOMAS NELSON
& ZONDERVAN

To my amazing mother,
May Olive Kohel.

Dreaming
that
the Spirit
will
blow freely
in me
is my wish.

Bluebird in Apple Blossoms
Watercolor 2021

Realizing
feelings
of being linked
to others
and nature
is profound.

Angel Falls, Venezuela
Watercolor 2019

Imagining
the
unimaginable,
the
unfathomable,
and the
limitless
for my
boundaries.

Tulip Passion
Watercolor 2022

Changing
allows room
for
any enrichment
or
tuning when
another treasure
is found.

Sleeping Fawn
Watercolor 2016

Developing
my divinity
must
be a way that
feels good
and uplifting
to me.

Iris I
Watercolor 2011

Offering
*a gift
is part
of the person
who gives it
and is a way
of saying
"I love you."*

Ruby-Throated Hummingbird, Male
Watercolor 2019

Accepting
a gift
allows
the giver
to become
part
of our lives.

Ruby-Throated Hummingbird, Female
Watercolor 2019

Forgiving
others
becomes natural
when
you have been
forgiven.

Texas Hill Country
Watercolor 2019

Succeeding
depends
on finding what
I love to do and
putting forth my
efforts.

Hibiscus II
Watercolor 2017

Achieving
my goal
takes
self-motivation
and
determination.

Pink Oleander
Watercolor 2015

Fulfilling
my life
requires
my
involvement
in the whole
of living.

Prime Yellow Rose
Watercolor 2021

Complimenting
individuals
increases their
positiveness
toward themselves
and others.

Bird of Paradise
Watercolor 2015

Believing
in
someone
can
completely turn
that person
toward success
and
happiness.

Resplendent Quetzal
Watercolor 2019

Trusting
can be
developed
by showing
expectation
and belief
in someone.

Lake Geneva, Switzerland
Watercolor 2021

Challenging
others
to realize
their abilities
and
creativity
is a joy.

Clematis Jackmanii
Watercolor 2020

Belonging
helps
us feel
accepted
and
together
with others.

My Rose
Watercolor 2011

Smiling
gives us
a bright outlook
and
is good
for our
health and mood.

Mockingbird in Yaupon Holly
Watercolor 2017

Encouraging
and
inspiring others
can give them
hope
and confidence.

El Páramo – Merida, Venezuela
Watercolor 2021

Anticipating
brings me
hope
for the
future.

Isla de Margarita, Venezuela
Watercolor 2021

Apologizing
must come from
my heart
and
show empathy
to the one
I hurt.

Peach Time
Watercolor 2016

Cooperating
with
another
individual
always makes
the
job easier.

Roadside Coreopsis
Watercolor 2020

Completing my goals gives me a sense of accomplishment.

Wild Roses
Watercolor 2016

Exploring
provides me
with new
opportunities
to know
our world
better.

Wild Cosmos
Watercolor 2021

Breathing
deeply
helps us
relax our bodies
and minds
as well as
appreciate
the
present moment.

Cedar Waxwing
Watercolor 2018

Accepting
others
is clearly
love
in practice.

Red Oak Leaves
Watercolor 2012

Celebrating
*helps us
enjoy
the goodness
of life.*

Male Bobwhite Quail
Watercolor 2020

Laughing
lightens my day,
connects me
with others,
and helps me
forgive.

Bobwhite Quail Bevy
Watercolor 2020

Discovering
new things
makes us
feel good and
allows our minds
to expand.

Dune Grass-Tasmania, Australia
Watercolor 2022

Hoping
and cherishing
a desire
keeps us in
an anticipatory
mood.

Maple Leaves
Watercolor 2012

Thanking
and praising
others
can change lives
as it increases
self-worth.

Ring-Necked Pheasant, Male
Watercolor 2022

Listening
well
encourages
the speaker
to feel value,
acceptance,
and trust.

Sumac Leaves I
Watercolor 2012

Adapting
gives me
something to use
for
a new purpose.

Double Red Poinsettia
Watercolor 2011

Tolerating
and
accepting others,
whatever
may be their
differences,
is my goal.

Winter Cardinal
Watercolor 2016

Expressing
the joy
of my spirit
makes me
feel alive.

Whitetail Yearling
Watercolor 2019

Enduring
stress when
difficulties arise
helps me
through the day.

Winter Woods King
Watercolor 2021

Praying
is a part
of life itself;
pray
your feelings
and
ask for grace.

Pink Poinsettia
Watercolor 2010

Delighting
in
each other
and ourselves
is pleasing
to our Creator.

Tasman Sea Sunset I
Watercolor 2017

Printed in the United States
by Baker & Taylor Publisher Services